The Musician's Book Of the Mass

John Hajda and Diana M. Kaulback

Resource Publications, Inc.
San Jose, California

© 2000 Resource Publications, Inc. All rights reserved.
No part of this book may be photocopied or otherwise
reproduced without permission from the publisher.
For reprint permission, write to:

Reprint Department
Resource Publications, Inc.
160 E. Virginia Street #290
San Jose, CA 95112-5876

Library of Congress Cataloging in Publication Data

Hajda, John, 1964–
   The musician's book of the mass / by John Hajda and
Diana M. Kaulback.
      p. cm.
   ISBN 0-89390-481-3 (pbk.)
     1. Church music—Catholic Church—Instruction and
study. 2. Choirs (Music) 3. Mass (Music) 4. Catholic
Church—Liturgy—Study and teaching. I. Kaulback, Diana,
1969– II. Title

MT88.H26 2000
264'.0202—dc21   99-059953

00 01 02 03 04 | 5 4 3 2 1

Editorial director: Nick Wagner
Production coordinator: Mike Sagara
Production assistant: Terri All
Copyeditor: Robin Witkin

Contents

To Music Directors, Liturgists, and Clergy . . . 5

Chapter 1
Holy 10
A Holy People 11

Chapter 2
Holy Times 18

Chapter 3
Holy Music 26

Chapter 4
Holy Preparation 32
For Rehearsal
For Mass
Prayer

Chapter 5
Order of the Mass. 40
  Gathering Rites
  Liturgy of the Word
  Liturgy of the Eucharist (Preparation Rites)
  Liturgy of the Eucharist (Eucharistic Prayer)
  Liturgy of the Eucharist (Communion Rite)
  Concluding Rites

Chapter 6
Putting It Together 48
  Moving Forward

Appendix
Blessing of Music Ministers 52
  Celebration of the Word of God
  to Bless Ministers of Music

Suggested Reading
for Additional Study 60

To Music Directors, Liturgists, and Clergy

> Servers, readers, commentators, and members of the choir also exercise a genuine liturgical function. ... They must all be deeply imbued with the spirit of the liturgy, in the measure proper to each one, and *they must be trained to perform their functions in a correct and orderly manner* (*Constitution on the Sacred Liturgy* 29, emphasis added).

The purpose of this book is to help you train your musicians as liturgical ministers. It is divided into six chapters. Each chapter can be treated as an independent lesson that should take no more than twenty minutes to complete. Because the lessons are independent, you can conduct your training as

TO MUSIC DIRECTORS, LITURGISTS, AND CLERGY

part of a half-day retreat or at six consecutive music rehearsals.

Each lesson contains material about the liturgy that all church musicians should know. Because we do not assume that your choir members are familiar with technical liturgical terminology, such as "progressive solemnity," important concepts are described with nontechnical, easy-to-understand language. At the end of each lesson, we provide three questions for the reader. These questions are not test questions. Rather, they are designed to help the musician consider how she or he can become a better *liturgical minister*. For each chapter, we encourage you to have each member of your music team read a paragraph, give your musicians a few moments to consider their answers to the questions at the end of the chapter, then ask your musicians to share their answers to these questions with each other.

In addition to learning about their holy (i.e., special) role, your musicians will better understand the role of music and the different types of music leadership in the liturgy. They will learn the musical roles of everyone else involved in the liturgies, including the presider and the assembly. Finally, they will learn about the purposes of liturgical music, the flow of the liturgical year, and the musical elements of the liturgy. At the end of the book is a blessing liturgy that you can use to help your community

TO MUSIC DIRECTORS, LITURGISTS, AND CLERGY

recognize your music team's achievement and commitment to its ministry.

Much of the material for this book comes from four main church documents: *Constitution on the Sacred Liturgy, Music in Catholic Worship, Liturgical Music Today,* and *Environment and Art in Catholic Worship*. You should have these documents available for the musicians who might be interested in learning even more about music ministry. Additional material comes from articles in the newsletter *Simple Gifts: Better Liturgical Music on a Smaller Budget* (Resource Publications, Inc.). Perhaps most important, we have tapped into our combined experience of thirty-seven years as music directors for volunteer Catholic choirs.

This book is a part of a series of training aids for those who engage in special ministry roles in the Catholic liturgy. The other books are *Young Server's Book of the Mass* by Kenneth Guentert, *The Usher's Book of the Mass* by the editors of *Ministry & Liturgy* magazine, and *Liturgical Ministry*. All of the books in this series are published by Resource Publications, Inc., and can be ordered by calling toll-free in the United States (888) 2RES-PUB.

Acknowlegdments

Some of the material from Chapter 1 and 2 is based on *Young Server's Book of the Mass*. The scripted liturgy for the blessing of music ministers

TO MUSIC DIRECTORS, LITURGISTS, AND CLERGY

is adapted from "Order for the Blessing of Altar Servers, Sacristans, Musicians, and Ushers" in *Book of Blessings* (New York: Catholic Book Publishing Co., 1989, Chap. 62).

Chart on page 34 created by Donald Neuen, director of choral activities at UCLA. For more information on this chart and vowel shaping, please see Mr. Neuen's book, *Choral Concepts*, available in Fall 2000 and published by Schirmer Books.

Chapter 1

Holy

In this book, we will often use the word *holy*. We do not intend this word to mean "angelic" or "blessed" or "sacred." In Hebrew, the word *kodesh* means "holy" in the sense of "set aside" or "special." You are holy in that sense because, as a member of the music group, you have assumed a leadership role in the liturgical ministry of your community.

A Holy People

"You are 'a chosen race, a royal priesthood, a holy nation, a people of his own, so that you may announce the praises' of him who called you out of darkness into his wonderful light" (1 Pt 2:9 NAB). You are part of that "holy nation." This does not mean that you are better than people who do not go to your church or who do not believe in your God. It means that you are part of a special community, one special to God, with special responsibilities to serve God and your neighbors.

As a music minister, you are "holy" in another way. You have a special role to play—you help the rest of the assembly sing the acclamations, psalms, hymns, and other musical prayers in the Mass. You help to build the body of Christ by your presence and by the ways that you encourage everyone's participation. You help to make the liturgy more beautiful, more special, more "holy." A wise person once said that the one who sings well, prays twice. As a music minister, you are a *professor* of faith, not a *performer*.

Everyone who is present at the liturgy has a special (holy) role when it comes to music:

- The **liturgical assembly** is the gathering of believers who sing, listen, and pray. These people are the Church. The assembly has the primary role, which is to actively participate in the liturgy in a full and conscious manner. There is no audience, no passive element in the celebrations of the Church.

The people who fill the following roles are also part of the assembly. At certain times during the liturgy, they come forward from the assembly to carry out important functions that the assembly needs in order to pray well together.

- The **presider** is the one who leads the gathered assembly in prayer. There are a number of liturgical elements that he should sing. He should always sing along with the assembly.

- The **music director** prepares and leads the music. She or he must be knowledgeable of both music and the liturgy. In addition, the music director may take a prominent role in the planning of the music, decide on repertoire, tend to the public address system, be responsible for the recruitment of new choir members, and serve in other ways on your parish ministry team.

- The **cantor** leads the assembly in sung prayer, often during the singing of the responsorial psalm but during other moments as well. The cantor may intone (sing) a melody and gesture to the assembly to repeat the tune. In many communities, the cantor teaches new music before liturgy begins.

- The **choir**, like the cantor, also leads the assembly in sung prayer. The choir may also alternate a musical passage with the assembly. By rehearsing harmony parts and working on special musical skills like phrasing and blend, the choir helps to make the music of the Mass more beautiful. Sometimes—but not too often!—the choir will sing a piece by themselves. The choir pieces are not performances; they are a special way of proclaiming our faith in and praise to God.

- During sung music, the **instrumentalists** provide the foundation for the voices by providing the proper starting pitch, introducing the tempo and style, and playing the introductions so everyone knows when to start singing. At certain times, the **instrumentalists** provide musical support, such as an instrumental piece before Mass, an instrumental underscore to a spoken text, or a recessional piece.

Your community has other people with special roles in the music ministry. The **planning committee** may work with the presider and music director to plan and evaluate the liturgies. The **director of worship** or **liturgy director** may oversee the music ministry in addition to other liturgical ministries such as lectors and communion ministers. The **director of religious education** and the **catechists** teach and model the value of musical participation in those who are preparing for the sacraments or those who are learning more about the Catholic faith. The **ushers** are responsible for hospitality and the distribution of hymnals or song sheets to the assembly.

As you can see, every person has a role in the music of your church's liturgies. As a member of the music ministry team, you are a leader among ministers.

Questions for Reflection and Discussion

1. Why did I join my church's music group or choir?

2. How have I benefited from being a member of the group?

3. What can I do *this week* to better encourage the participation of the assembly?

CHAPTER 1

Prayer

Holy God, you give us the gift of music so that we may praise you. Thank you for calling us to special roles in the ministry of the Church. Help us to realize our gifts and develop them to their fullest, so that we may do our part in building the Body of Christ. Amen.

Chapter 2

Holy Times

The Catholic community gathers for worship at special times. The most special of these times is Sunday, which is the day that Jesus rose from the dead. So every Sunday, we remember Jesus' death and resurrection.

But every Sunday is not the same. Like winter, spring, summer, and fall, the church has different seasons throughout the year. In fact, the church year does not begin on January 1. Instead, the church follows its own calendar:

- **Advent** is the beginning of the church year. It starts on the Sunday closest to November 30. It is a time during which we prepare for Christmas and for the Second Coming of Christ. There are always four Sundays during the Advent season.

- **Christmas** lasts for more than one day. It extends from the Christmas Eve Masses to the Sunday after January 6. During Christmas, we celebrate the birth of Christ, his youth, and his life up until his baptism by John.

- The winter portion of **Ordinary Time** fills in the space between Christmas and Lent. We call it "ordinary" because these are the times during which we count the weeks, all the way up to the 33rd or 34th Sunday of Ordinary Time. These types of numbers are also known as "ordinal" numbers. Ordinary Time is not a season but a way of making time between seasons. It does not have a specific focus, but rather celebrates the life and ministry of Christ and his followers. The majority of the church year is spent in Ordinary Time.

- **Lent** begins on Ash Wednesday and continues until the beginning of the Mass of the Lord's Supper on Holy Thursday. Lent prepares us for Easter; it is also the final period of preparation for those who will be initiated at the Easter Vigil. Although it is a time for more intense prayer, fasting, and other sacrifices, Lent is not supposed to be gloomy or depressing. It is penitential, meaning we examine our lives and look for the ways in which we as individuals and as a church community do not live up to the vows of our baptism. We help each other live more faithfully to our baptismal commitment as an example to the catechumens and the elect, always remembering God's mercy and forgiveness. Lent does not, however, have the exuberance of Easter or Christmas.

- The **Easter Triduum** is the most holy time of the entire church year. From the Mass of the Lord's Supper on Holy Thursday to the Good Friday service to the Easter Vigil and Easter Sunday through Sunday Evening Prayer, Christians celebrate the passion, death, and resurrection of Christ. The high point of the Triduum is the Easter Vigil, when we celebrate our salvation and incorporate new members into the church.

HOLY TIMES

- Like Christmas, **Easter** lasts for more than one day. The Easter season extends from Easter Sunday to Pentecost, fifty days later. During this time, we celebrate Christ's resurrection from the dead, his time spent among the disciples after his resurrection, his ascension into heaven, and the gift of the Holy Spirit. We also assist the neophytes (those who were initiated at the Easter Vigil) to reflect on the meaning and implications of their new life with the Church.

- The summer portion of **Ordinary Time** begins the day after Pentecost. Ordinary Time continues through the fall. The last Sundays of Ordinary Time focus on the Second Coming of Christ. Appropriately, the final Sunday of Ordinary Time—and the church year—is the Solemnity of Christ the King.

Throughout the church year, there are other special days called "holy days." These are days when the entire assembly is called to worship. In the United States, these days are:

- The Assumption of Mary (August 15)
- All Saints (November 1)

CHAPTER 2

- The Immaculate Conception of Mary (December 8)
- Christmas (December 25)
- The Solemnity of Mary, the Mother of God (January 1)
- The Ascension of Our Lord (a Thursday, forty days after Easter Sunday. In the western United States the Ascension is celebrated on the Seventh Sunday of Easter.)

It is interesting to note that Ash Wednesday is not specified as a holy day of obligation. Nevertheless, in many parishes the assembly is larger on Ash Wednesday than on some Sundays. Finally, some Sundays during Ordinary Time are set aside for special focuses, such as The Body and Blood of Christ or Christ the King.

Like the four seasons of the calendar year, the seasons of the church year each have their own special moods and colors. Music is one way that the moods of the church seasons are expressed. For example, in Advent, although we hear Christmas carols on the radio and watch Christmas specials on television, we do not sing Christmas carols at Mass. Instead, we sing songs about the coming of Christ, like "O Come, O Come, Emmanuel." During the Christmas season, when the stores have removed their Christmas merchandise, we sing Christmas songs until the second Sunday of January! Because Advent and Lent are penitential and preparatory, the Glory to God is not sung during these seasons, and no alleluias are sung during the period from Ash Wednesday up to the Easter Vigil. Your music director may change the settings of the Mass parts (e.g., penitential rite; Gospel acclamation; Holy, Holy, Holy; memorial acclamation; Great Amen; Lamb of God) at the beginning of a liturgical season. In these and other ways, music communicates the purpose and focus of each season of the church year.

Questions for Reflection and Discussion

1. What is my favorite season of the standard calendar year (winter, spring, summer, fall)? Why?

2. What is my favorite time of the church year (Advent, Christmas, Lent, Easter, and Ordinary Time)? Why?

3. How can I make the Easter Triduum a more holy time for me?

Prayer

God of all time, we celebrate the many facets of your love through the cycle of the church year. Help us to make each season special so that we may know you in every moment. Amen.

Chapter 3

Holy Music

No one knows when or why human beings first started making and appreciating music. However, since virtually every culture and subculture on earth makes music, we know that music is an important part of being human. In the Bible there are a number of references to music, such as the song that Moses, Miriam, and the Israelites sang to the Lord after they escaped the Pharaoh's army at the Red Sea (Ex 15:20–21), the Song of Judith (Jdt 15:14—16:1–17), and the Last Supper (Mk 14:26). In fact, the entire book of Psalms, or Psalter, is a collection of religious songs.

Music is special for a number of reasons. One reason is that music is a way to communicate. Without communication, human societies could not exist. Language also communicates, but music is different because it does not need words. Perhaps you have been moved emotionally by a musical piece or a special song. Maybe you have tried watching a scary movie or television show with the sound turned down; the show is much less scary! Many philosophers and others have struggled with why music can have such an impact, but, for our purposes, it is sufficient to know that music can intensify one's emotional experiences.

Liturgical music intensifies our *prayer* experience. Music helps us to express feelings about God and each other in ways that are difficult with words alone. We have seen a banner inside a church that read: "When words fail, music speaks." In most of the music during Mass we use words and music together to pray.

Liturgical music belongs to the *assembly*. That means it is the assembly who makes the music, not just the choir or the cantor or the musicians. We have music at Mass because it helps to bring everyone closer to each other and closer to God. Although concerts of inspirational music are popular, they do not have a place during Mass. The Mass has no audience, only participants. In this way, the Mass is different from almost any other type of public gathering.

Liturgical music serves the liturgical *texts*. For hundreds of years, there has been a tension between composers, who wanted to set the text of certain prayers in a musically challenging and artistic manner, and church leaders, who wanted the music to serve, not overtake, the text. All musicians should keep in mind that the music exists because the texts—the prayers, readings, and acclamations—exist. This means that composers should not change the meaning of the words in the parts of the Mass, arrangers should write vocal parts so that the words can still be understood by the assembly, instrumentalists and vocalists should not drown out the words that are sung by the assembly, and cantors and choir members should be certain that they sufficiently and properly enunciate the text. Imagine how different your prayer experience would be if you could not understand a word that the readers or presider were saying! The same principle holds true for liturgical music.

Liturgical music is a form of *catechesis*. Catechesis is the manner by which we learn our faith, so that we can live it. Liturgical music and how it is used at liturgy teach us that we have a relationship with God and with each other. We are not a room full of individuals each praying to God in his or her own private way. Rather, we are a community (an assembly) that gathers to listen to God's word, remember God's wonderful love for this "chosen race," and to respond in songs of praise, petition, and thanksgiving. The way we interact with each other through the spoken and sung dialogues, the hymns, and prayers shows us how we should live our lives outside of Mass—as people of thanksgiving who recognize and honor the holiness of every person. Both the music group and the assembly share equally important roles in the musical dialogue of the liturgy. In the same way, everyone plays an integral role in building the kingdom of God.

As a form of communication, as prayer, as an enhancement of the liturgical texts, and as a form of catechesis, music plays a special, holy part in the liturgy. Liturgical music is indeed very different from any other music in our daily lives.

Questions for Reflection and Discussion

1. What is my favorite liturgical song? What do I like the most about this song?

2. What is the text of my favorite liturgical song about? Why is it my favorite text?

CHAPTER 3

3. What is the role of the congregation in my favorite liturgical song? When this song is sung at my church, does the congregation participate fully in its role?

Prayer

God of sound and silence, you give us the gift of music so that we may express with our hearts that which we cannot express with words alone. Fill us with joy and open our mouths that we may always praise your name with the choirs of angels in heaven. Amen.

Chapter 4

Holy Preparation

Remember that you are first a member of the assembly and that your primary function in the liturgy is to participate fully with the rest of the assembly. This means that you are attentive to the readings, responding in the dialogues, participating in the gestures, and deeply involved in the silent prayer of the assembly. You may find that it is difficult to pray at a liturgy when you are worrying about what you are singing or playing. But by preparing well for your special role at Mass, you become more confident as a music minister so that you can participate better as an assembly member. Here are a few things you can do to prepare your role.

For Rehearsal

An integral part of your preparation is rehearsal with the other choir members, instrumentalists, and your music director. It is important for you to be at the rehearsal for any Mass at which you intend to sing or play. Usually your director will schedule a weekday rehearsal for the upcoming Sunday Mass. Although someone may be able to learn the music just before the Mass, the importance of the role of music deserves more time and commitment from each music minister to enable the music to inspire, nurture, and evoke the assembly's faith. Also, regular attendance at rehearsals will help you be more familiar with the music so that you can "pray" the music rather than just get through it at Mass. Be ready to work. Bring all your necessary sheet music, books, and binders. Arrive early to get settled and to arrange your music in order.

Usually, your music director will lead you through warm-up exercises at the beginning of each rehearsal. But there are a few things you can do on your own to help you warm up before. Stretch and loosen up your body. Making music, especially singing, involves your whole body, not just your voice. Stand, twist, stretch, bend, and shake out any tension in your arms, back, neck, and legs. A common mistake many singers make is to sing without opening their mouth enough to shape good vowels. Stretch your facial and lip muscles. If you are opening your mouth and shaping your vowels well, your lips and face may feel sore at first. But just like with any physical exercise, this soreness will go away with more use of those muscles. If you are an instrumentalist, warm up with a few scales and arpeggios. Do any breathing, lip, or finger exercises that you need to do to play your instrument well. Arrive early to tune up.

Two of the most important elements for good singing are breathing and vowel shaping. Your director may be able to suggest a breathing exercise for you to do at home to help increase your breath control using your diaphragm muscle. If you are sitting when you sing, keep your back and neck straight, hold your music up, and keep both feet flat on the floor. This will help you use your diaphragm muscle more efficiently. For vowel shaping, here's a simple chart to help you make better sounding vowels. For each vowel, make your lips into the corresponding shape while keeping the space inside your mouth large and open.

"Dark" Vowels

oo = ◯ (size of a dime)

oh = ◯ (size of a nickel)

aw = ◯ (size of a quarter)

"Bright" Vowels

ee = ▢ (box shape)

eh = ▯ (elongated)

ah = ▯ (more elongated)

Note: For the "bright" vowels, only a very small portion of the upper and lower teeth show between the lips. For these "bright" vowels, think more of using the teeth to shape the vowels rather than the lips.

Watch yourself in a mirror when you sing. Are you opening your mouth enough? Are you making the appropriate shape with your lips?

At the rehearsal, be attentive even when the director is rehearsing another vocal or instrumental section. Not only is this respectful to the other music ministers, but it will also help you be ready when the director calls upon your section. Always bring an eraser and a pencil (never a pen) to make notes in the music, because you probably won't remember every direction come Sunday. If your director allows it, tape-record the rehearsal so you can practice at home.

For Mass

During the week, read the Scripture readings for the Mass at which you are serving. You can find them in your church's missalette or Lectionary. Often, your parish bulletin will list the Bible passages for the upcoming week. Start with the Gospel reading followed by the first reading and the psalm. The Gospel will normally be the focus for the day while the first reading is related to the Gospel. The psalm usually will be a good summary of the sense of the readings. The second reading ordinarily is not thematically related to the other readings, though the homily, prayers, or hymns may pick up on some of its images. Reading the Scriptures for the day will help you participate more fully in the Mass, prepare you to hear the homily, and enable you to respond more consciously to the prayers.

Get plenty of rest the night before. On the day of Mass, warm up as you do for rehearsal. Have your music ready and in order before you arrive at the church. Double-check to be sure you've brought everything you may need (tissues, water, capo, extra strings, mute, extra reeds, guitar cables, cough drops, etc.). Dress as if you are prepared to do an important job—because you are! Some choirs will have you wear a robe. Be sure yours is clean and looking neat.

During the Mass, stay attentive to the liturgy. In many churches, the choir is visible to the assembly, and so any unnecessary talking or movement can be very distracting. That's why it's important to have your music ready and in order. After a piece, wait until an appropriate time to turn to the next piece of music. Avoid searching for music during moments when you, as an assembly member, should be praying (for example, when the presider says, "Let us pray"). When you are singing, have a pleasant expression on your face. Remember, you minister with your whole body, not just your voice. Make eye contact with the assembly and smile. It's true that you can hear a smile when you sing.

Prayer

The best way you can prepare for your role as a music minister is to pray. The music you make for worship is already prayer. But your own private personal prayer during the week strengthens the prayer you make with others. As a music minister, you are primarily encouraging, enabling, and enhancing the prayer of the assembly (that includes you!) through music and song. You are serving the assembly by helping them to express what they can't express with words alone. Remember you are a minister and not a performer. As a liturgical minister, the community has entrusted to you the responsibility of preparing and executing your role well so that the assembly can give glory to God. This is what makes you different from a singer or musician on a stage. The music you make is only a vehicle for something bigger and not an end in itself. Here's a prayer you can say by yourself or together at rehearsal or just before Mass to help calm any nerves and focus your mind and heart to the purpose of your special role.

God of song and silence,
we thank you for bringing us together this day
that we might praise you once again.
Send your Spirit upon us and breathe
   in us a word of life
that we might be ministers of prayer
   for this assembly
and messengers of your love to this world.
We ask this through Jesus Christ our
   Lord. Amen.

CHAPTER 4

Questions for Reflection and Discussion

1. What one thing can I work on this month or this year to improve my musical skills? Who or what resources will help me improve as a musician?

2. What are some things that help me pray during Mass when I am serving as a music minister? What are some things that distract me from prayer during Mass when I am serving?

3. What does it mean for me to be a music *minister*? How can I deepen my faith life so that my ministry is strengthened?

Prayer

God of peace and wisdom, you have called us to be special messengers of your Gospel. Focus our minds and calm our fears. Help us lovingly prepare for our ministry so that we may lead your people in praise of your holy name. Amen

Chapter 5

Order of the Mass

Gathering Rites

- Gathering Song and Procession
- Sign of the Cross and Greeting from the Presider
- Penitential Rite (Kyrie, or Lord have mercy, or "I confess …" or another formula)
- Glory to God
- Opening Prayer

These introductory rites are secondary to the Liturgy of the Word and the Liturgy of the Eucharist that follow. The Gathering Rites help to unify all these individual people into one worshiping body. It prepares the assembly to hear the Word and to celebrate the Eucharist. The gathering song and the opening prayer are the most important parts. The gathering song should be something that everyone can sing.

Liturgy of the Word

- First Reading (from Hebrew Scriptures or Acts of the Apostles)
- Psalm Response
- Second Reading (from the letters or the Book of Revelation)
- Gospel Acclamation
- Third Reading (from the Gospels)
- Homily
- Profession of Faith
- General Intercessions

In the Liturgy of the Word, God speaks to the assembly. The people are fed with the Word of God proclaimed in the readings and culminating in the Gospel and the homily. The assembly responds and accepts the Word through the psalm, Gospel acclamation, profession of faith, and intercessions. The psalm response is always sung. (The psalms were written as songs. They are never recited, just as you would never speak the words to "Happy Birthday.") The psalm is the assembly's response to the Word and so should be something that all can participate in. The Gospel acclamation serves to express the assembly's thanksgiving for the life-giving Word and again, should always be sung by the whole assembly.

Liturgy of the Eucharist (Preparation Rites)

- Setting the table
- Procession and song
- Prayers over the bread and wine
- Mingling of water and wine
- Prayer of the priest (said softly)
- Washing of hands
- Prayer over the Gifts

Like the Gathering Rites, this section of the Liturgy of the Eucharist is mainly preparatory. It is basically like setting the table for a meal. It serves to prepare the bread and wine for the Eucharist. The most important parts are the bringing up of bread and wine, placing them on the altar, and the prayer over them. A song may accompany the procession, but is not necessary. (Don't make this simple secondary rite more important than it really is by doing an elaborate piece for the procession.)

Liturgy of the Eucharist (Eucharistic Prayer)

- Preface
- Holy
- Consecration and story
- Memorial Acclamation (remembering Christ's death, resurrection, and second coming)
- Anamnesis (remembering)
- Intercessions and commemorations
- Great Amen

The Eucharistic Prayer is the heart of the whole Mass. It is a prayer of thanksgiving and blessing that is lead by the presider on behalf of the assembly. The assembly affirms and assents to the prayer through the acclamations of the Sanctus (Holy), Memorial Acclamation, and the Great Amen. The importance of this prayer and the need for strong responses by the assembly require that the acclamations be sung, and if possible, the words of the prayer by the presider. The Great Amen should be just that—great! It is the assembly's "yes" to the entire prayer.

CHAPTER 5

Liturgy of the Eucharist (Communion Rite)

- Lord's Prayer
- Rite of Peace
- Fraction Rite (Breaking of Bread) and Lamb of God
- Invitation to Communion
- Sharing of Communion and Communion Song
- Silent Prayer or Song of Thanksgiving
- Prayer after Communion

The sharing of bread and wine is the climax of the Mass. It is the Body and Blood of Christ (the assembly) being fed by the Body and Blood of Christ (consecrated bread and wine) so that they may in turn be the Body and Blood of Christ for the world. The most important music piece of this rite is the Communion song. It should express the unity of the assembly with Christ and with each other. Because the assembly is in procession during the song, it is best to use a piece that has a memorable refrain that the assembly can sing without the use of a hymnal. The time after communion is reserved for silent prayer or a communal song of thanksgiving, *not* a meditation song performed by the choir or a soloist.

The assembly has just been united as intimately as can be with each other and with Christ. It is not a time for private personal prayer. Even the silent prayer is meant to be a communal act during which the entire assembly is united through prayer in thanksgiving to God.

Concluding Rites

- Final Blessing
- Dismissal
- Recession of Ministers
- Closing Song (optional)

This final section is again secondary. The important part is the dismissal that commands the assembly to "go, love and serve the Lord." It is strange to give the assembly the command to go, but then ask them to stay and sing one final song. That is why the closing song is considered optional. An instrumental piece might be more appropriate.

Questions for Reflection and Discussion

1. How do I help the community gather for Mass and become an assembly? Which songs in our repertoire are sung well by the whole assembly?

2. What is the high point of the Mass for me? Why? Is there any point in the Mass when I "tune out" or am bored? What can I do to be more present throughout the Mass?

3. What parts of the Mass does our community do well? Why do these parts work? What parts of the Mass do we need to improve? How can our ministry help to improve these parts?

Prayer

God who was, who is, and who is to come, you call us each week to the table of your Word and Eucharist to be fed. Help us recognize the importance of this Sunday gathering so that we can recommit our lives to be your body and blood for the life of the world. Amen.

Chapter 6

Putting It Together

To be an effective music minister, you must be both a good liturgist and a good musician. But sometimes there is a conflict between good liturgy and good music. For example, great music—in the sense of a virtuoso or difficult performance—does not necessarily make great liturgy. This is what makes liturgical music different from other types of music. Lets's review some of the special features that make liturgical music unique.

- Liturgical music helps the assembly participate actively in a full and conscious manner.

- Liturgical music expresses the seasons of the church year, so that different aspects of our faith and salvation are made clear.

- Liturgical music is a special form of prayer, by which members of the assembly communicate with God and with each other.

- Liturgical music requires careful preparation, rehearsal, and execution.

- Liturgical music has a variety of functions (call to unity, response to a reading, acclamation) during Mass. Not every moment during Mass requires singing. However, the acclamations should always be sung.

Moving Forward

The completion of liturgical minister training will help you serve God and God's people better. But this is just the beginning of your commitment to your ministry, a ministry that is essential to a holy, meaningful worship experience.

We encourage you to seek a more active role in your music ministry. This role can take many forms: participation in liturgy planning, assisting the music director in preparing music for rehearsal or worship aids, setting up and taking down equipment before and after Mass, or planning social functions for the music group.

We also encourage you to constantly develop your skills as a liturgist, minister, and musician. Congratulations on finishing a major step in that

CHAPTER 6

development. Now the rest is up to you, your sister and brother ministers, and God.

Questions for Reflection and Discussion

1. As I review my answers to the questions at the end of the previous units, would I answer any of them differently now?

2. What can I do in the next month to take a more active role in my church's music ministry?

3. What will I do next to develop my skills as a liturgist, minister, and musician?

Prayer

Loving God, our service as music ministers is a gift of love to you and your people. Continue to bless our ministry, and help us to develop our skills so that we can praise you to the fullest of our abilities. Amen.

Appendix

Blessing Of Music Ministers

Once you have completed these chapters and other sufficient training for this ministry, it is appropriate for your community to bless you as you begin or continue your work as music ministers. Ideally this would take place at a Sunday liturgy, perhaps at which other ministers are also being blessed. (See *Book of Blessings,* chapter 62 [New York: Catholic Book Publishing Co., 1989], for the "Order of Blessing of Musicians" within a Mass.) However, be sure to consider the liturgical season and the particular Sunday that is being celebrated. For example, it would be inappropriate to celebrate this blessing during Lent or on a Sunday that already has a special rite or event, such as the rite of acceptance or baptism of infants. It would be more appropriate to do the blessing during Ordinary Time, or on a Sunday during Easter, or on the feast day of the community's patron saint. Also consider what the assigned readings are for that Sunday or feast. The blessing would work best if the readings spoke of ministry and service or music and praise and other related ideas. Based on the assigned readings, here are some appropriate Sundays for this blessing to take place and the related readings for that Sunday:

2nd Sunday Easter Cycle A
   (Acts 2:42–47)

3rd Sunday Easter Cycle C
   (Rv 5:11–14)

Pentecost Sunday Cycle A, B, C
   (1 Cor 12:3–7,12–13)

2nd Sunday Ordinary Time Cycle A
   (Is 49:3, 5–6; Ps 40)

2nd Sunday Ordinary Time Cycle B
   (1 Sm 3:3–10,19; Ps 40)

2nd Sunday Ordinary Time Cycle C
   (Ps 96; 1 Cor 12:4–11)

3rd Sunday Ordinary Time Cycle C
   (1 Cor 12:12–30; Lk 1:1–4,14–21)

4th Sunday Ordinary Time Cycle C
   (Ps 71; 1 Cor 12:31—13:13)

APPENDIX

5th Sunday Ordinary Time Cycle C
(Is 6:1–2,3–8; Ps 138)

8th Sunday Ordinary Time Cycle B
(2 Cor 3:1–6)

15th Sunday Ordinary Time Cycle C
(Dt 30:10–14)

20th Sunday Ordinary Time Cycle B
(Eph 5:15–20)

22nd Sunday Ordinary Time Cycle B
(Jas 1:17–18,21–22,27)

26th Sunday Ordinary Time Cycle A
(Phil 2:1–11)

27th Sunday Ordinary Time Cycle A
(Phil 4:6–9)

27th Sunday Ordinary Time Cycle C
(2 Tm 1:6–8,13–14)

29th Sunday Ordinary Time Cycle A
(Ps 96; 1 Thes 1:1–5)

Other appropriate times would be at a Liturgy of the Word service during the week, perhaps at a choir rehearsal or at a community event such as a banquet or concert. It could be done around the feast of St. Cecilia (November 22), one of the patron saints of music. It would be important to have a representative number of the community there for the blessing. If possible, the pastor would preside. A script for the blessing of music ministers outside of Mass follows.

Celebration of the Word of God to Bless Ministers of Music

Gathering Song

Sign of the Cross

> Presider: In the name of the God whose word brings life, in the name of the God whose Spirit brings fire, in the name of the Father, (+) and of the Son, and of the Holy Spirit.
> *Amen.*

Greeting

> Presider: The grace and favor of our Lord Jesus Christ be with you always.
> *And also with you.*

Introduction

> Presider or other minister: Our baptism calls each of us to serve as members of the Body of Christ. Some of us are called to serve as ministers of the liturgical assembly. Today, we give thanks to God for our brothers and sisters who have heard and answered God's call to serve as ministers of musical prayer. We ask God to bless them abundantly as they begin/continue their liturgical ministry in our community.

APPENDIX

Opening Prayer

> Presider: Let us pray.
> Lord of unending joy,
> be close to those who call upon you.
> Fill our hearts and open our mouths,
> that with the angels and saints in heaven
> who sing your praise,
> we may proclaim your wonderful deeds
> to all your people.
> We ask this through Christ our Lord.
> *Amen.*

Reading *(proclaimed by a lector of the community)*: Colossians 3:12–17

Psalm *(choose one to sing)*:

> Psalm 22
> Psalm 40
> Psalm 66
> Psalm 71
> Psalm 81
> Psalm 89
> Psalm 96
> Psalm 138
> Psalm 145

> Reflection: The presider or other suitable minister (perhaps the choir director) may give a brief reflection on the reading and psalm to prepare the assembly to celebrate the following blessing.

BLESSING OF MUSIC MINISTERS

Intercessions *(It is appropriate to have the intercessions chanted and the response sung.)*

> Presider: God provides for all our needs. Let us pray for these music ministers that God may bless them in their service to our community.
>
> Reader: For the Church and this community of N.: may all God's people continue to be generous in their service to each other and to the world. We pray to the Lord.
>
> Reader: For all who serve God's people in the courts of this assembly: may their love for God and neighbor continue to shine and give glory to God's name. We pray to the Lord.
>
> Reader: For these ministers who have been chosen and called by God and this community to serve as musicians and singers for liturgical service: may the music they make lift our hearts to give constant praise to God. We pray to the Lord.
>
> Presider: Whatever we do, in word or in deed, let us do in the name of the Lord Jesus, through whom we are able to call God, Father.
>
> *(Lord's Prayer is chanted.)*

Prayer of Blessing *(The music ministers to be blessed are invited to stand before the assembly. Assembly members standing closest to them may lay their hands upon the shoulders of these ministers. Other assembly members lay their hands upon the person in front of them. Thus, the whole assembly is connected through touch in the blessing of the ministers. The following prayer may be used, or a song of blessing may be sung by the entire assembly.)*

Presider:
    Loving Creator,
        whom saints and angels delight to
        worship in heaven:
    Be ever present with your servants
        who seek through music to perfect
        the praises offered by your people
        on earth.
    Bless these brothers and sisters
        who have answered your call to service
        and commit themselves to the needs
        of this community.
    Fill their ministry
        with the fire of your Holy Spirit
        that hearts may be lifted up in praise
        and lives transformed
        by the beauty of their work.
    Grant us even now,
        glimpses of your beauty,
        and make us worthy to
        behold it unveiled forevermore.

BLESSING OF MUSIC MINISTERS

We ask this through Christ our Lord.
Amen.

Concluding Blessing

Presider: Lord God,
you have clothed us with your love
through the gift of our baptism.
Bless us in our work
of building up the Body of Christ
and keep us ever in your love.

And may almighty God bless you,
the Father, and the Son, (+) and the
Holy Spirit. *Amen.*

Song of Praise

Suggested Reading For Additional Study

Bernadin, Cardinal Joseph. *Guide for the Assembly.* Chicago: Liturgy Training Publications, 1997.

Huck, Gabe. *Liturgy with Style and Grace.* Chicago: Liturgy Training Publications (800-933-1800), 1984.

Johnson, Lawrence J. *The Word and Eucharist Handbook.* San Jose: Resource Publications, Inc. (888-273-7782), 1993.

The Liturgy Documents: A Parish Resource. Chicago: Liturgy Training Publications, 1991.

Mahony, Cardinal Roger. *Gather Faithfully Together: A Guide for Sunday Mass.* Chicago: Liturgy Training Publications, 1997.

Ministry & Liturgy magazine. San Jose: Resource Publications, Inc.

Pastoral Music magazine. National Association of Pastoral Musicians (202-723-5800).

Simple Gifts newsletter. San Jose: Resource Publications, Inc.

More resources for musicians

THE LITURGICAL MUSIC ANSWER BOOK: ML Answers the 101 Most-Asked Questions

Peggy Lovrien

Paper, 160 pages, 5.5" x 8.5", 0-89390-454-6

Here is a virtual training manual for music directors, song leaders, and choir members. *The Liturgical Music Answer Book* helps parish liturgical music committees study the liturgical music documents of the church, discover the appropriate ways to choose music for the liturgy, and operate with confidence in their ministry as liturgical musicians.

The convenient question and answer format makes this material quickly accessible to busy liturgical musicians. From the basic, "Why do we sing at Mass?" to the practical, "What is the best way to introduce a new song?" to the specific, "Why are seat cushions bad for liturgical music?" — music committees will find satisfying answers to their nagging liturgical music questions.

EVALUATING YOUR LITURGICAL MUSIC MINISTRY

Keith L. Patterson

Paper, 160 pages, 8½" x 11", ISBN:0-89390-258-6

Find out how effective your church's liturgical music program really is. The author includes all the information you need for surveying and measuring the quality and effectiveness of your present liturgical music, then guides you in implementing the changes necessary to improve your church's worship experience.

Liturgical Music

RETURN, RENEW & REMEMBER

Julie & Tim Smith

Cassette (10 Compositions)
Songbook (Keyboard, Guitar, Choir, C-Instrument, Reproducible Congregational Parts)

Return, Renew and Remember; Building Up the Body of Christ; This Cup - Psalm 116; Celebrate Life; Lord, Let Your Mercy Be Upon Us - Psalm 33; Let Us Rejoice - An Easter Proclamation; Do This in Memory of Me; Share the Message; Challenged and Chosen; Welcome to the Family.

I WILL SING/CANTARÉ
Psalms in English and Spanish

Julie & Tim Smith

Cassette (13 Compositions), UPC 784967-0012-48
Songbook, ISBN 0-89390-410-4 Religion/Music/Liturgy, Guitar/keyboard arrangements, 3- and 4-part vocals,Composer notes, Assembly lead lines

This unique collection of liturgical music provides the music minister with added flexibility. These engaging melodies can be sung in English only, Spanish only, or in English and Spanish. Texts have been carefully written to adhere to the natural rhythms and accents of the two spoken languages as well as to the original meaning of the liturgical texts. It uses a call-and-response technique that makes assembly participation a snap — even without pre-Mass practice!

More Liturgical Music

A EUCHARISTIC PEOPLE

Julie & Tim Smith

Cassette (14 compositions)
Songbook (Keyboard, Guitar, 2- & 3-part Choir)

Make Us a Eucharistic People; Because We Are God's Chosen Ones; Who Do You Say That I Am?; Drawn to the Water; We Are Called to Serve; God Revealed; The Mass Never Ends; Everybody Get Ready; Signs of Your Coming; To the Creator; In My Very Being; People of Passion; Ordinary Holiness; Ain't Nothin' Gonna Hold Me.

SINGING MORNING & EVENING PRAYER

John Hajda

Double Cassette
Songbook (Guitar, Lead Vocal)

Includes Dialogs, Hymns, Canticles, Intercessions, settings for The Lord's Prayer and Psalms for Morning and Evening Prayer.

Order from your local bookseller, or contact:

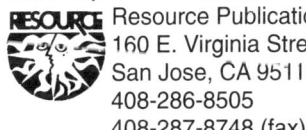
Resource Publications, Inc.
160 E. Virginia Street #290
San Jose, CA 95112-5076
408-286-8505
408-287-8748 (fax)
888-273-7782 (toll free, 8-5 PT)
www.rpinet.com

Resources for Music Ministry

When it comes to good assembly singing, you don't need lots of hardware. You need focus. And know-how. That's where SIMPLE GIFTS comes in. You'll learn how to focus on the assembly — and how to take advantage of tunes that are familiar and easy to sing. Each issue is packed with tips and practical ideas you can put to use in your choir and assembly today. To subscribe, complete and return the form below.

❏ Yes, I want to try SIMPLE GIFTS! Please send my first issue right away. I will receive the next issue of SIMPLE GIFTS followed by an invoice. If I like what I see, I'll return the invoice with a $24 check (for foreign orders add $5 for postage) and receive the remaining five issues. If I choose not to subscribe, I'll mark "cancel" on the invoice and return it. The first issue is mine to keep.

NAME:_____

PARISH:_____

ADDRESS:_____

CITY/STATE:_____

ZIP:_____

PHONE: (_____) _____
Mail this form to: Simple Gifts
160 East Virginia Street #290
San Jose, CA 95112-5876

(408) 286-8505, toll free (888) 273-7782
FAX: (408) 287-8748, www.rpinet.com